MVFOL

The Best Slow Cooker Recipes

Publications International, Ltd.
Favorite Brand Name Recipes at www.fbnr.com

Pictured on the front cover *(clockwise from top right):* Cajun-Style Country Ribs *(page 88)*, Caribbean Sweet Potato & Bean Stew *(page 26)*, Slow Cooker Steak Fajitas *(page 96)* and Three-Bean Mole Chili *(page 6)*.
Pictured on the back cover: Italian-Style Sausage with Rice *(page 84)*.

ISBN-13: 978-1-4127-2657-3
ISBN-10: 1-4127-2657-3

Manufactured in China.

8 7 6 5 4 3 2 1

Preparation/Cooking Times: Preparation times are based on the approximate amount of time required to assemble the recipe before cooking, baking, chilling or serving. These times include preparation steps such as measuring, chopping and mixing. The fact that some preparations and cooking can be done simultaneously is taken into account. Preparation of optional ingredients and serving suggestions is not included.

CONTENTS

SOUPS, STEWS & CHILIS

Three-Bean Mole Chili

Prep Time: *10 minutes* / **Cook Time:** *5 to 6 hours*

1 can (15 ounces) pinto beans, rinsed and drained
1 can (15 ounces) chili beans in spicy sauce, undrained
1 can (15 ounces) black beans, rinsed and drained
1 can (14½ ounces) Mexican or chili-style diced tomatoes, undrained
1 large green bell pepper, diced
1 small onion, diced
½ cup beef, chicken or vegetable broth
¼ cup prepared mole paste*
2 teaspoons ground cumin
2 teaspoons chili powder
2 teaspoons minced garlic
2 teaspoons ground coriander (optional)
   Toppings: crushed tortilla chips, chopped fresh cilantro or shredded
   cheese

Mole paste is available in the Mexican section of large supermarkets or in specialty markets.

Slow Cooker Directions

1. Combine beans, tomatoes with juice, bell pepper, onion, broth, mole, cumin, chili powder, garlic and coriander, if desired, in slow cooker; mix well.

2. Cover; cook on LOW 5 to 6 hours or until vegetables are tender.

3. Place toppings in small bowls. Serve hot chili with toppings.

Makes 4 to 6 servings

Simple Turkey Soup

2 pounds ground turkey, cooked and drained
1 can (28 ounces) whole tomatoes, undrained
2 cans (14 ounces each) beef broth
1 bag (16 ounces) frozen mixed soup vegetables (such as carrots, beans, okra, corn or onion)
½ cup uncooked barley
1 teaspoon salt
1 teaspoon dried thyme leaves
½ teaspoon ground coriander
Black pepper

Slow Cooker Directions
Combine all ingredients in slow cooker. Add water to cover. Cover; cook on HIGH 3 to 4 hours or until barley and vegetables are tender.

Makes 8 servings

COOK'S TIP

This soup is very easy to make! Try adding other frozen or canned vegetables or diced potatoes. Sliced, diced or stewed tomatoes can be substituted for the whole tomatoes. For a large crowd, add corn and serve with corn bread.

Simple Turkey Soup

Rustic Vegetable Soup

1 jar (16 ounces) picante sauce
1 package (10 ounces) frozen mixed vegetables, thawed
1 package (10 ounces) frozen cut green beans, thawed
1 can (10 ounces) condensed beef broth, undiluted
1 to 2 baking potatoes, cut into ½-inch pieces
1 medium green bell pepper, chopped
½ teaspoon sugar
¼ cup finely chopped fresh parsley

Slow Cooker Directions
Combine all ingredients except parsley in slow cooker. Cover; cook on LOW 8 hours or on HIGH 4 hours. Stir in parsley; serve.   *Makes 8 servings*

Easy Corn Chowder

Prep Time: *15 minutes* / **Cook Time:** *7 to 8 hours*

2 cans (14½ ounces each) chicken broth
1 bag (16 ounces) frozen corn kernels
3 small potatoes, peeled and cut into ½-inch pieces
1 red bell pepper, diced
1 medium onion, diced
1 rib celery, sliced
½ teaspoon salt
½ teaspoon black pepper
¼ teaspoon ground coriander
½ cup heavy cream
8 slices bacon, crisp-cooked and crumbled (optional)

Slow Cooker Directions
1. Place broth, corn, potatoes, bell pepper, onion, celery, salt, black pepper and coriander into slow cooker. Cover; cook on LOW 7 to 8 hours.

2. Partially mash soup mixture with potato masher to thicken. Stir in cream; cook on HIGH, uncovered, until hot. Adjust seasonings, if desired. Garnish with bacon, if desired.   *Makes 6 servings*

Rustic Vegetable Soup

Red Bean Soup with Andouille Sausage

2 tablespoons unsalted butter

1 large onion, diced

3 stalks celery, diced

2 large cloves garlic, chopped

1 ham hock

8 cups chicken stock

1½ cups dried red kidney beans, soaked in cold water 1 hour, rinsed and drained

1 bay leaf

1 pound andouille smoked sausage or other pork sausage, cut into ½-inch pieces

1 sweet potato, diced

2 parsnips, diced

Salt and black pepper to taste

Slow Cooker Directions

1. Melt butter in large saucepan over medium heat. Add onion, celery and garlic. Cook and stir 5 minutes; add to slow cooker along with ham hock, chicken stock, kidney beans and bay leaf. Cover; cook on HIGH 2 hours.

2. Remove ham hock and discard. Cover; cook 2 hours more.

3. Add sausage, potato and parsnips. Cover; cook 30 minutes more or until kidney beans are soft. Season with salt and pepper.   *Makes 6 to 8 servings*

Note: Use a 6-quart slow cooker for this recipe. If using a smaller slow cooker, cut recipe ingredients in half.

Red Bean Soup with Andouille Sausage

Mushroom Barley Stew

Prep Time: *10 minutes* / **Cook Time:** *6 to 7 hours*

1 tablespoon olive oil
1 medium onion, finely chopped
1 cup chopped carrots (about 2 medium carrots)
1 clove garlic, minced
1 cup uncooked pearl barley
1 cup dried wild mushrooms, broken into pieces
1 teaspoon salt
½ teaspoon dried thyme leaves
½ teaspoon black pepper
5 cups vegetable broth

Slow Cooker Directions

1. Heat oil in medium skillet over medium-high heat. Add onion, carrots and garlic; cook and stir 5 minutes or until tender. Place in slow cooker.

2. Add barley, mushrooms, salt, thyme and pepper to slow cooker. Stir in broth.

3. Cover; cook on LOW 6 to 7 hours. Adjust seasonings, if desired.

Makes 4 to 6 servings

COOK'S TIP

To turn this thick robust stew into a soup,
add 2 to 3 additional cups of broth.
Cook the same length of time.

Mushroom Barley Stew

Double-Hearty, Double-Quick Veggie Chili

2 cans (15½ ounces each) dark kidney beans, rinsed and drained

1 package (16 ounces) frozen bell pepper stir-fry mixture *or* 2 bell peppers, chopped

1 cup frozen corn kernels

1 can (14½ ounces) diced tomatoes with peppers, celery and onions, undrained

3 tablespoons chili powder or to taste

2 teaspoons sugar

2 teaspoons ground cumin, divided

½ teaspoon salt

1 tablespoon extra virgin olive oil

Sour cream (optional)

Chopped fresh cilantro (optional)

Slow Cooker Directions

1. In colander, combine beans, bell pepper mixture and corn. Run under cold water until beans and vegetables are well rinsed. Shake off excess water; place in slow cooker. Add tomatoes with juice, chili powder, sugar and 1½ teaspoons cumin.

2. Cover; cook on LOW 5 hours or on HIGH 3 hours.

3. Stir in salt, remaining ½ teaspoon cumin and olive oil. Serve with sour cream and cilantro, if desired.   *Makes 4 to 6 servings*

Note: If using fresh bell peppers, add 1 small onion, chopped.

Double-Hearty, Double-Quick Veggie Chili

Mediterranean Lentil Soup

2 tablespoons olive oil

1 large onion, diced

1 stalk celery, chopped

2 large cloves garlic, finely minced

1 can (28 ounces) peeled whole plum tomatoes, drained and chopped

1½ cups dried lentils, soaked in cold water 1 hour, rinsed and drained*

1 tablespoon tomato paste

1½ teaspoons dried thyme leaves

6 cups beef broth

2 bay leaves

Vinaigrette

¾ cup packed fresh basil leaves

⅓ cup olive oil

2 tablespoons minced fresh parsley leaves

2 tablespoons red wine vinegar

Salt and black pepper to taste

Add 1 to 2 hours to cooking time if you do not soak lentils before cooking.

Slow Cooker Directions

1. Place all ingredients except vinaigrette in slow cooker. Stir to combine; cover and cook on LOW 8 hours or on HIGH 4 hours or until lentils are soft.

2. While soup is simmering, prepare vinaigrette. Combine basil, ⅓ cup olive oil, parsley and vinegar in blender or food processor. Process on high speed until smooth. Stir vinaigrette into soup just before serving. Season with salt and pepper. *Makes 4 to 6 servings*

Mediterranean Lentil Soup

Peppery Potato Soup

Prep Time: *15 minutes* / **Cook Time:** *6 to 8 hours*

2 cans (14½ ounces each) chicken broth
4 small baking potatoes, halved and sliced
1 large onion, quartered and sliced
1 rib celery with leaves, sliced
¼ cup all-purpose flour
¾ teaspoon black pepper
½ teaspoon salt
1 cup half-and-half
1 tablespoon butter
   Celery leaves and fresh parsley (optional)

Slow Cooker Directions

1. Combine broth, potatoes, onion, celery, flour, pepper and salt in slow cooker; mix well. Cover; cook on LOW 6 to 7½ hours.

2. Stir in half-and-half; cover and continue to cook 1 hour.

3. Remove slow cooker lid. Slightly crush potato mixture with potato masher. Continue to cook, uncovered, an additional 30 minutes until slightly thickened. Just before serving, stir in butter. Garnish with celery leaves and parsley, if desired.   *Makes 6 (1¼-cup) servings*

Peppery Potato Soup

Winter's Best Bean Soup

Prep Time: *15 minutes* / **Cook Time:** *8 hours*

    6 ounces bacon, diced
   10 cups chicken broth
    3 cans (15 ounces each) Great Northern beans, drained
    1 can (14½ ounces) diced tomatoes, undrained
    1 package (10 ounces) frozen sliced or diced carrots
    1 large onion, chopped
    2 teaspoons minced garlic
    1 fresh rosemary sprig *or* 1 teaspoon dried rosemary leaves
    1 teaspoon black pepper

Slow Cooker Directions

1. Cook bacon in medium skillet over medium-high heat just until cooked; drain and transfer to slow cooker. Add remaining ingredients.

2. Cover; cook on LOW 8 hours or until beans are tender. Remove rosemary sprig and mince leaves before serving.   *Makes 8 to 10 servings*

Slow Cooker Cheese Soup

    4 cups (16 ounces) shredded Cheddar cheese
    2 cans (10¾ ounces each) condensed cream of celery soup, undiluted
    1 teaspoon paprika
    1 teaspoon Worcestershire sauce
 1¼ cups half-and-half
    Salt and black pepper

Slow Cooker Directions

1. Combine cheese, soup, paprika and Worcestershire sauce in slow cooker.

2. Cover; cook on LOW 2 to 3 hours.

3. Add half-and-half; stir to combine. Cover; cook another 20 minutes. Season with salt and pepper to taste. Garnish as desired.   *Makes 4 servings*

Winter's Best Bean Soup

Lamb Stew

1 large onion, chopped

2 to 3 tablespoons plus 1½ teaspoons bacon fat or olive oil, divided

½ cup all-purpose flour

2 teaspoons salt

1 teaspoon black pepper

3 pounds boneless lamb for stew, cut into 2- to 2½-inch pieces

2 tablespoons sugar, divided

3 cans (14½ ounces each) beef broth

3 tablespoons tomato paste

4 cloves garlic, chopped

1 tablespoon dried thyme leaves

1 tablespoon fresh chopped rosemary leaves

2 bay leaves

1 pound carrots, peeled and cut into 2-inch chunks

1 pound petite Yukon gold potatoes, halved

1 package (10 ounces) frozen peas

Slow Cooker Directions

1. Cook and stir onion in 1½ teaspoons bacon fat in large skillet over medium heat until golden. Add to slow cooker.

2. Mix flour with salt and pepper in large bowl. Dredge lamb in flour mixture. Heat 1 tablespoon bacon fat in skillet over medium-high heat until hot. Add half of lamb to skillet; cook until browned on all sides. Add 1 tablespoon sugar; mix well to coat meat. Cook several minutes, until meat is caramelized. Add meat to slow cooker. Repeat with remaining lamb, using remaining 1 to 2 tablespoons bacon fat as needed and remaining 1 tablespoon sugar.

3. Add broth to skillet and boil over high heat, scraping sides and bottom of pan to loosen browned bits. Add tomato paste, garlic, thyme, rosemary and bay leaves. Stir to combine. Pour over meat mixture in slow cooker. Cover; cook on LOW 4 hours or on HIGH 2 hours.

4. Add carrots and potatoes. Cover; cook 3 to 4 hours more on LOW or 1½ to 2½ hours on HIGH or until vegetables and lamb are tender.

5. Add peas. Cook 30 minutes more. Remove and discard bay leaves before serving. *Makes 6 to 8 servings*

French Onion Soup

4 tablespoons butter
3 pounds yellow onions, sliced
1 tablespoon sugar
2 to 3 tablespoons dry white wine or water (optional)
8 cups beef broth
8 to 16 slices French bread
½ cup shredded Gruyère or Swiss cheese

Slow Cooker Directions

1. Melt butter in large skillet over medium to low heat. Add onions; cover and cook just until onions are limp and transparent, but not browned, about 10 minutes.

2. Remove cover. Sprinkle sugar over onions. Cook, stirring, until onions are caramelized, 8 to 10 minutes. Scrape onions and any browned bits into slow cooker. If desired, deglaze pan by adding wine to pan, returning to heat, bringing to a boil and scraping up any browned bits with a wooden spoon. Add to slow cooker with onions. Stir in broth. Cover; cook on LOW 8 hours or on HIGH 6 hours.

3. Preheat broiler. To serve, ladle soup into individual soup bowls; top with 1 or 2 slices bread and about 1 tablespoon cheese. Place under broiler until cheese is melted and bubbly.   *Makes 8 servings*

Variation: Substitute 2 cups dry white wine for beef broth.

Caribbean Sweet Potato & Bean Stew

Prep Time: *10 minutes /* **Cook Time:** *5 to 6 hours*

2 medium sweet potatoes (about 1 pound), peeled and cut into 1-inch cubes
2 cups frozen cut green beans
1 can (15 ounces) black beans, rinsed and drained
1 can (14½ ounces) vegetable broth
1 small onion, sliced
2 teaspoons Caribbean or Jamaican jerk seasoning
½ teaspoon dried thyme leaves
¼ teaspoon salt
¼ teaspoon ground cinnamon
⅓ cup slivered almonds, toasted*
    Hot pepper sauce (optional)

To toast almonds, spread in single layer on baking sheet. Bake in preheated 350°F oven 8 to 10 minutes or until golden brown, stirring frequently.

Slow Cooker Directions

1. Combine sweet potatoes, beans, broth, onion, jerk seasoning, thyme, salt and cinnamon in slow cooker.

2. Cover; cook on LOW 5 to 6 hours or until vegetables are tender.

3. Adjust seasonings. Serve with almonds and hot pepper sauce, if desired.

Makes 4 servings

Caribbean Sweet Potato & Bean Stew

SIDE DISHES

Peasant Potatoes

¼ cup (½ stick) unsalted butter

1 large onion, chopped

2 large cloves garlic, chopped

½ pound smoked beef sausage, cut into ¾-inch slices

1 teaspoon dried oregano leaves

6 medium potatoes, preferably Yukon Gold, cut into 1½- to 2-inch pieces
   Salt and black pepper

2 cups sliced Savoy or other cabbage

1 cup diced or sliced roasted red bell pepper

½ cup shaved fresh Parmesan cheese

Slow Cooker Directions

1. Melt butter in large skillet over medium heat. Add onion and garlic. Cook and stir 5 minutes or until onion is transparent. Stir in sausage and oregano; cook 5 minutes. Stir in potatoes, salt and black pepper until well blended. Transfer mixture to slow cooker.

2. Cover; cook on LOW 6 to 8 hours or on HIGH 3 to 4 hours, stirring every hour if possible. During last 30 minutes of cooking, add cabbage and bell pepper.

3. Sprinkle with Parmesan cheese just before serving.   *Makes 6 servings*

Winter Squash and Apples

1 butternut squash (about 2 pounds), peeled, seeded and cut into 2-inch
    pieces
2 apples, cored and cut into slices
1 medium onion, quartered and sliced
    Salt and black pepper
1½ tablespoons butter

Slow Cooker Directions

1. Place squash in slow cooker. Add apples and onion. Sprinkle with salt and black pepper; stir well. Cover; cook on LOW 6 to 7 hours.

2. Before serving, stir in butter and season with additional salt and pepper, if desired. *Makes 4 to 6 servings*

New England Baked Beans

4 slices uncooked bacon, chopped
3 cans (15 ounces each) Great Northern beans, rinsed and drained
¾ cup water
1 small onion, chopped
⅓ cup canned diced tomatoes, well drained
3 tablespoons *each* packed light brown sugar, maple syrup and
    unsulphured molasses
2 cloves garlic, minced
½ teaspoon *each* salt and dry mustard
⅛ teaspoon black pepper
1 bay leaf

Slow Cooker Directions

1. Cook bacon in large skillet until almost cooked but not crispy. Drain on paper towels.

2. Combine bacon and remaining ingredients in slow cooker. Cover; cook on LOW 6 to 8 hours or until onion is tender and mixture is thickened. Remove bay leaf before serving. *Makes 4 to 6 servings*

Winter Squash and Apples

Spanish Paella-Style Rice

Prep Time: *10 minutes* / **Cook Time:** *4½ hours*

2 cans (14½ ounces each) chicken broth
1½ cups converted long grain rice, uncooked (not quick cooking or
      instant rice)
1 small red bell pepper, diced
⅓ cup dry white wine or water
½ teaspoon powdered saffron *or* ½ teaspoon turmeric
⅛ teaspoon red pepper flakes
½ cup frozen peas, thawed
   Salt

Slow Cooker Directions

1. Combine broth, rice, bell pepper, wine, saffron and red pepper flakes in slow cooker; mix well.

2. Cover; cook on LOW 4 hours or until liquid is absorbed.

3. Stir in peas. Cover; cook on LOW 15 to 30 minutes longer or until peas are hot. Season with salt.   *Makes 6 servings*

Variations: Add ½ cup cooked chicken or ham cubes, shrimp or quartered marinated artichokes, drained, at the same time the peas are added.

COOK'S TIP

Paella is a Spanish dish of saffron-flavored
rice combined with a variety of meats,
seafood and vegetables. Paella is traditionally
served in a wide, shallow dish.

Spanish Paella-Style Rice

Eggplant Italiano

Prep Time: *10 minutes* / **Cook Time:** *3½ to 6 hours*

1¼ pounds eggplant, cut into 1-inch cubes
2 medium onions, thinly sliced
2 ribs celery, cut into 1-inch pieces
1 can (16 ounces) diced tomatoes, undrained
3 tablespoons tomato sauce
1 tablespoon olive oil
½ cup pitted ripe olives, cut in half
2 tablespoons balsamic vinegar
1 tablespoon sugar
1 tablespoon capers, drained
1 teaspoon dried oregano or basil leaves
Salt and black pepper to taste
Fresh basil leaves, leaf lettuce and red jalapeño pepper* (optional)

Jalapeño peppers can sting and irritate the skin; wear rubber gloves when handling peppers and do not touch eyes. Wash hands after handling.

Slow Cooker Directions

1. Combine eggplant, onions, celery, tomatoes with juice, tomato sauce and oil in slow cooker. Cover; cook on LOW 3½ to 4 hours or until eggplant is tender.

2. Stir in olives, vinegar, sugar, capers and oregano. Season with salt and black pepper. Cover; cook 45 minutes to 1 hour or until heated through. Garnish with basil, lettuce and jalapeño pepper, if desired.   *Makes 6 servings*

No-Fuss Macaroni & Cheese

Prep Time: *10 minutes* / **Cook Time:** *2 to 3 hours*

  2 cups (about 8 ounces) uncooked elbow macaroni
  4 ounces pasteurized processed cheese, cubed
  1 cup (4 ounces) shredded mild Cheddar cheese
  ½ teaspoon salt
  ⅛ teaspoon black pepper
1½ cups milk

Slow Cooker Directions

Combine macaroni, cheeses, salt and pepper in slow cooker. Pour milk over top. Cover; cook on LOW 2 to 3 hours, stirring after 20 to 30 minutes.

Makes 6 to 8 servings

Variation: Stir in desired vegetable.

COOK'S TIP

As with all macaroni and cheese dishes, as it sits, the cheese sauce thickens and begins to dry out. If it dries out, stir in a little extra milk and heat through. Do not cook longer than 4 hours.

Orange-Spiced Sweet Potatoes

    2 pounds sweet potatoes, peeled and diced
    ½ cup (1 stick) butter, cut into small pieces
    ½ cup packed dark brown sugar
    1 teaspoon ground cinnamon
    1 teaspoon vanilla
    ½ teaspoon ground nutmeg
    ½ teaspoon orange zest
      Juice of 1 medium orange
    ¼ teaspoon salt
      Chopped, toasted pecans (optional)

Slow Cooker Directions
Place all ingredients in slow cooker, except pecans. Cover; cook on LOW
4 hours or on HIGH 2 hours or until potatoes are tender. Sprinkle with pecans
before serving, if desired. *Makes 8 (½-cup) servings*

Variation: Mash potatoes with a hand masher or electric mixer; add ¼ cup
milk or cream for a moister consistency. Sprinkle with a cinnamon-sugar
mixture.

Scalloped Tomatoes & Corn

Prep Time: *7 minutes* / **Cook Time:** *4 to 6 hours*

    1 can (15 ounces) cream-style corn
    1 can (14½ ounces) diced tomatoes, undrained
    ¾ cup saltine cracker crumbs
    1 egg, lightly beaten
    2 teaspoons sugar
    ¾ teaspoon black pepper

Slow Cooker Directions
Combine all ingredients in slow cooker; mix well. Cover; cook on LOW 4 to
6 hours. *Makes 4 to 6 servings*

Orange-Spiced Sweet Potatoes

MAIN ENTRÉES

Honey-Mustard Chicken Wings

Prep Time: *20 minutes* / **Cook Time:** *4 to 5 hours*

  3 pounds chicken wings
  1 teaspoon salt
  1 teaspoon black pepper
  ½ cup honey
  ½ cup barbecue sauce
  2 tablespoons spicy brown mustard
  1 clove garlic, minced
  3 to 4 thin lemon slices

Slow Cooker Directions

1. Rinse chicken and pat dry. Cut off wing tips; discard. Cut each wing at joint to make two pieces. Sprinkle salt and pepper on both sides of chicken. Place wing pieces on broiler rack. Broil 4 to 5 inches from heat about 10 minutes, turning halfway through cooking time. Place broiled chicken wings in slow cooker.

2. Combine honey, barbecue sauce, mustard and garlic in small bowl; mix well. Pour sauce over chicken wings. Top with lemon slices. Cover; cook on LOW 4 to 5 hours.

3. Remove and discard lemon slices. Serve wings with sauce.

Makes about 24 wings

Pork Roast Landaise

2 tablespoons olive oil

2½ pounds boneless center cut pork loin roast

   Salt and black pepper

1 medium onion, diced

2 large cloves garlic, minced

2 teaspoons dried thyme leaves

2 cups chicken broth or stock, divided

2 tablespoons cornstarch or arrowroot

¼ cup sugar

¼ cup red wine vinegar

½ cup port or sherry wine

2 parsnips, cut into ¾-inch-thick slices

3 pears, cored and cut into ¾-inch-thick slices

1½ cups pitted prunes

Slow Cooker Directions

1. Heat olive oil in large saucepan over medium-high heat. Season pork roast with salt and pepper; brown in saucepan on all sides. Transfer browned roast to slow cooker.

2. Blend ¼ cup chicken broth and cornstarch in small bowl until smooth; set aside.

3. Add onion and garlic to saucepan; cook and stir over medium heat for 2 to 3 minutes. Stir in thyme. Add onion mixture to slow cooker.

4. In same saucepan combine sugar and vinegar. Cook over medium heat, stirring constantly, until mixture becomes syrupy. Add port; cook 1 minute more. Add remaining 1¾ cups chicken broth. Stir cornstarch mixture; whisk into broth mixture. Cook and stir until smooth and slightly thickened. Pour into slow cooker.

5. Cover; cook on LOW 8 hours or on HIGH 4 hours. During last 30 minutes of cooking, add parsnips, pears and prunes.   *Makes 4 to 6 servings*

Serving Suggestion: Serve over rice or mashed potatoes or with French bread to dunk in the gravy.

Pork Roast Landaise

Slow Cooker Brisket of Beef

1 whole well-trimmed beef brisket (about 5 pounds)
2 teaspoons bottled minced garlic
½ teaspoon black pepper
2 large onions, cut into ¼-inch slices and separated into rings
1 bottle (12 ounces) chili sauce
12 ounces beef broth, dark ale or water
2 tablespoons Worcestershire sauce
1 tablespoon packed brown sugar

Slow Cooker Directions

1. Place brisket, fat side down, in slow cooker. Spread garlic evenly over brisket; sprinkle with pepper. Arrange onions over brisket. Combine chili sauce, broth, Worcestershire sauce and brown sugar; pour over brisket and onions. Cover; cook on LOW 8 hours.

2. Turn brisket over; stir onions into sauce and spoon over brisket. Add vegetables, if desired. Cover; cook until fork-tender. Transfer brisket to cutting board. Tent with foil; let stand 10 minutes.*

3. Stir juices in slow cooker. Spoon off and discard fat from juices. (Juices may be thinned to desired consistency with water or thickened by simmering, uncovered, in saucepan.) Carve brisket across grain into thin slices. Spoon juices over brisket.   *Makes 10 to 12 servings*

*At this point, brisket may be covered and refrigerated up to one day before serving. To reheat brisket, cut diagonally into thin slices. Place brisket slices and juice in large skillet. Cover; cook over medium-low heat until heated through.

Variation: Stir diced red boiling potatoes, cut carrots, sliced parsnips or turnips into juices during last hour of cooking time.

Slow Cooker Brisket of Beef

Italian-Style Pot Roast

Prep Time: *15 minutes* / **Cook Time:** *8 to 9 hours*

2 teaspoons minced garlic

1 teaspoon salt

1 teaspoon dried basil leaves

1 teaspoon dried oregano leaves

¼ teaspoon red pepper flakes

1 boneless beef bottom round rump or chuck shoulder roast (about 2½ to 3 pounds)

1 large onion, quartered and thinly sliced

1½ cups prepared tomato-basil or marinara pasta sauce

2 cans (16 ounces each) Great Northern or cannellini beans, rinsed and drained

¼ cup shredded fresh basil or chopped Italian parsley (optional)

Slow Cooker Directions

1. Combine garlic, salt, basil, oregano and red pepper flakes in small bowl; rub over roast.

2. Place half of onion slices into slow cooker. Cut roast in half to fit into slow cooker. Place one half of roast over onion slices; top with remaining onion slices and other half of roast. Pour pasta sauce over roast. Cover; cook on LOW 8 to 9 hours or until roast is fork tender.

3. Remove roast from cooking liquid; tent with foil. Let liquid in slow cooker stand 5 minutes to allow fat to rise. Skim off fat.

4. Stir beans into liquid. Cover; cook on HIGH 10 to 15 minutes or until beans are hot. Carve roast across grain into thin slices. Serve with bean mixture and garnish with fresh basil, if desired.   *Makes 6 to 8 servings*

Italian-Style Pot Roast

Meatballs in Burgundy Sauce

60 frozen prepared fully-cooked meatballs
3 cups chopped onions
1½ cups water
1 cup red wine
2 packages (about 1 ounce each) beef gravy mix
¼ cup ketchup
1 tablespoon dried oregano leaves
1 package (8 ounces) curly noodles

Slow Cooker Directions

1. Combine meatballs, onions, water, wine, gravy mix, ketchup and oregano in slow cooker; stir to blend.

2. Cover; cook on HIGH 5 hours.

3. Meanwhile cook noodles according to package directions. Serve meatballs over noodles.

Makes 6 to 8 servings

Sweet and Spicy Sausage Rounds

1 pound Kielbasa sausage, cut into ¼-inch rounds
⅔ cup blackberry jam
⅓ cup steak sauce
1 tablespoon prepared mustard
½ teaspoon ground allspice
Hot cooked rice
Chopped green onions

Slow Cooker Directions

1. Place all ingredients in slow cooker; toss to coat completely. Cook on HIGH 3 hours or until thickly glazed.

2. Serve over rice tossed with chopped green onions.

Makes 3 cups

Meatballs in Burgundy Sauce

Greek-Style Chicken

Prep Time: *15 minutes* / **Cook Time:** *5 to 6 hours*

6 boneless skinless chicken thighs
½ teaspoon salt
½ teaspoon black pepper
1 tablespoon olive oil
½ cup chicken broth
1 lemon, thinly sliced
¼ cup pitted kalamata olives
1 clove garlic, minced
½ teaspoon dried oregano leaves
  Hot cooked orzo or rice

Slow Cooker Directions

1. Remove visible fat from chicken; sprinkle chicken thighs with salt and pepper. Heat oil in large skillet over medium-high heat. Brown chicken on all sides. Place in slow cooker.

2. Add broth, lemon, olives, garlic and oregano to slow cooker.

3. Cover; cook on LOW 5 to 6 hours or until chicken is tender. Serve with orzo. *Makes 4 to 6 servings*

Greek-Style Chicken

Ale'd Pork and Sauerkraut

1 jar (32 ounces) sauerkraut, undrained
1 tablespoon plus 1½ teaspoons sugar
1 can (12 ounces) dark beer or ale
3½ pounds boneless pork shoulder or pork butt roast
½ teaspoon salt
¼ teaspoon *each* garlic powder and black pepper
 Paprika

Slow Cooker Directions

1. Place sauerkraut in slow cooker. Sprinkle sugar evenly over sauerkraut; pour beer over all. Place pork, fat side up, on top of sauerkraut mixture; sprinkle evenly with remaining ingredients.

2. Cover; cook on HIGH 6 hours.

3. Remove pork to serving platter; arrange sauerkraut around pork. Spoon cooking liquid over sauerkraut. *Makes 6 to 8 servings*

Lemon-Thyme Beef with Beans

1 beef chuck roast (about 3 pounds), trimmed and cut into 2-inch pieces
2 cans (15 ounces each) white or pinto beans, rinsed and drained
1 can (15 ounces) red kidney beans, rinsed and drained
1 cup beef broth
1 medium onion, chopped
2 cloves garlic, minced
1 teaspoon *each* salt, grated lemon peel, dried thyme leaves and black pepper
 Chopped fresh parsley (optional)

Slow Cooker Directions

1. Place all ingredients, except parsley, in slow cooker. Cover; cook on LOW 8 to 9 hours or until beef is tender.

2. Adjust seasonings before serving, if desired. Arrange beef on top of beans. Garnish with parsley, if desired. *Makes 6 to 8 servings*

Ale'd Pork and Sauerkraut

Saucy Tropical Turkey

Prep Time: *15 minutes* / **Cook Time:** *6½ to 7½ hours*

3 to 4 turkey thighs, skin removed (about 2½ pounds)
2 tablespoons vegetable oil
1 small onion, halved and sliced
1 can (20 ounces) pineapple chunks, drained
1 red bell pepper, cubed
⅔ cup apricot preserves
3 tablespoons soy sauce
1 teaspoon grated lemon peel
1 teaspoon ground ginger
¼ cup cold water
2 tablespoons cornstarch
  Hot cooked rice

Slow Cooker Directions

1. Rinse turkey and pat dry. Heat oil in large skillet; brown turkey on all sides. Place onion in slow cooker. Transfer turkey to slow cooker; top with pineapple and bell pepper.

2. Combine preserves, soy sauce, lemon peel and ginger in small bowl; mix well. Spoon over turkey. Cover; cook on LOW 6 to 7 hours.

3. Remove turkey from slow cooker; keep warm. Blend water and cornstarch until smooth; stir into slow cooker. Cook on HIGH 15 minutes or until sauce is slightly thickened. Adjust seasonings. Return turkey to slow cooker; cook until hot. Serve with rice. *Makes 6 servings*

Saucy Tropical Turkey

Italian-Style Sausage with Rice

1 pound mild Italian sausage links, cut into 1-inch pieces
1 can (15 ounces) pinto beans, rinsed and drained
1 cup pasta sauce
1 green bell pepper, cut into strips
1 small onion, halved and sliced
½ teaspoon salt
¼ teaspoon black pepper
   Hot cooked rice

Slow Cooker Directions

1. Brown sausage in large skillet over medium heat. Pour off drippings. Place all ingredients except rice into slow cooker. Cover; cook on LOW 4 to 6 hours.

2. Serve with rice.   *Makes 4 to 5 servings*

Sweet and Sour Cabbage Borscht

2 pounds boneless beef chuck roast, cut into 4 pieces
1 can (28 ounces) whole tomatoes, cut into pieces, undrained
1 can (15 ounces) tomato sauce
1 large onion, thinly sliced
3 carrots, shredded
2 pounds green cabbage, shredded
4 cups water
¾ cup sugar
½ cup lemon juice
1 tablespoon caraway seeds
2 teaspoons salt
1 teaspoon black pepper

Slow Cooker Directions

1. Place all ingredients into slow cooker. Cover; cook on LOW 6 to 8 hours or until meat is tender.

2. Remove beef from slow cooker; shred. Return to slow cooker; mix well.
                                                    Makes 8 to 10 servings

Italian-Style Sausage with Rice

Southwestern Stuffed Peppers

Prep Time: *15 minutes* / **Cook Time:** *4 to 6 hours*

4 green bell peppers
1 can (16 ounces) black beans, rinsed and drained
1 cup (4 ounces) shredded pepper-Jack cheese
¾ cup medium salsa
½ cup frozen corn
½ cup chopped green onions with tops
⅓ cup uncooked long grain converted rice
1 teaspoon chili powder
½ teaspoon ground cumin
Sour cream (optional)

Slow Cooker Directions

1. Cut thin slice off top of each bell pepper. Carefully remove seeds, leaving pepper whole.

2. Combine remaining ingredients except sour cream in medium bowl. Spoon filling evenly into each pepper. Place peppers in slow cooker.

3. Cover; cook on LOW 4 to 6 hours. Serve with dollop of sour cream, if desired.   *Makes 4 servings*

Southwestern Stuffed Peppers

Cajun-Style Country Ribs

Prep Time: *15 minutes* / **Cook Time:** *6 to 8 hours*

2 cups baby carrots
1 large onion, coarsely chopped
1 large green bell pepper, cut into 1-inch pieces
1 large red bell pepper, cut into 1-inch pieces
2 teaspoons minced garlic
6 teaspoons Cajun or Creole seasoning, divided
3½ to 4 pounds pork country-style ribs
1 can (14½ ounces) stewed tomatoes, undrained
2 tablespoons water
1 tablespoon cornstarch
Hot cooked rice

Slow Cooker Directions

1. Place carrots, onion, bell peppers, garlic and 2 teaspoons Cajun seasoning in slow cooker; mix well.

2. Trim excess fat from ribs. Cut into individual ribs. Sprinkle 3 teaspoons Cajun seasoning over ribs; place in slow cooker over vegetables. Pour tomatoes with juice over ribs. (Slow cooker will be full.) Cover; cook on LOW 6 to 8 hours or until ribs are fork tender.

3. Remove ribs and vegetables from cooking liquid to serving platter. Let liquid stand 5 minutes to allow fat to rise. Skim off fat. Blend water, cornstarch and remaining 1 teaspoon Cajun seasoning. Stir into liquid in slow cooker. Cook on HIGH until sauce is thickened. Return ribs and vegetables to sauce; carefully stir to coat. Serve with rice. *Makes 6 to 8 servings*

Cajun-Style Country Ribs

SANDWICHES & WRAPS

Slow Cooker Steak Fajitas

Prep Time: *20 minutes* / **Cook Time:** *6 to 7 hours*

1 beef flank steak (about 1 pound), cut lengthwise in half, then crosswise into thin strips
1 medium onion, cut into strips
½ cup medium salsa
2 tablespoons fresh lime juice
2 tablespoons chopped fresh cilantro
2 cloves garlic, minced
1 tablespoon chili powder
1 teaspoon ground cumin
½ teaspoon salt
1 small green bell pepper, cut into strips
1 small red bell pepper, cut into strips
   Flour tortillas, warmed
   Additional salsa

Slow Cooker Directions

1. Combine steak, onion, ½ cup salsa, lime juice, cilantro, garlic, chili powder, cumin and salt in slow cooker.

2. Cover; cook on LOW 5 to 6 hours. Add bell peppers. Cover; cook on LOW 1 hour.

3. Serve with tortillas and additional salsa.   *Makes 4 servings*

Barbecued Beef Sandwiches

Prep Time: *20 to 25 minutes* / **Cook Time:** *8½ to 10½ hours*

3 pounds boneless beef chuck shoulder roast, cut in half
2 cups ketchup
1 medium onion, chopped
¼ cup cider vinegar
¼ cup dark molasses
2 tablespoons Worcestershire sauce
2 cloves garlic, minced
½ teaspoon salt
½ teaspoon dry mustard
½ teaspoon black pepper
¼ teaspoon garlic powder
¼ teaspoon red pepper flakes
Sesame seed sandwich buns, split

Slow Cooker Directions

1. Place roast in slow cooker. Combine ketchup, onion, vinegar, molasses, Worcestershire, garlic, salt, mustard, black pepper, garlic powder and red pepper flakes in large bowl. Pour sauce mixture over roast. Cover; cook on LOW 8 to 10 hours or on HIGH 4 to 5 hours.

2. Remove roast from sauce; cool slightly. Trim and discard excess fat from beef. Using two forks, shred meat.

3. Let sauce stand 5 minutes to allow fat to rise. Skim off fat.

4. Return shredded meat to slow cooker. Stir meat to evenly coat with sauce. Adjust seasonings, if desired. Cover; cook on LOW 15 to 30 minutes or until hot.

5. Spoon filling into buns and top with additional sauce, if desired.

Makes 12 servings

Barbecued Beef Sandwich

Hot & Juicy Reuben Sandwiches

Prep Time: *25 minutes* / **Cook Time:** *7 to 9 hours*

1 mild-cure corned beef (about 1½ pounds), trimmed of excess fat
2 cups sauerkraut, drained
½ cup beef broth
1 small onion, sliced
1 clove garlic, minced
¼ teaspoon caraway seeds
4 to 6 peppercorns
8 slices pumpernickel or rye bread
4 slices Swiss cheese
   Mustard

Slow Cooker Directions

1. Place corned beef, sauerkraut, broth, onion, garlic, caraway seeds and peppercorns in slow cooker.

2. Cover; cook on LOW 7 to 9 hours.

3. Remove beef from slow cooker. Cut across the grain into ¼-inch-thick slices. Divide evenly on 4 slices bread. Top each slice with ½ cup drained sauerkraut mixture and one slice cheese. Spread mustard on remaining 4 bread slices. Close sandwich. *Makes 4 servings*

Note: This two-fisted stack of corned beef, sauerkraut and melted Swiss cheese makes a glorious sandwich you'll want to serve often.

Hot & Juicy Reuben Sandwich

Brats in Beer

Prep Time: *5 minutes* / **Cook Time:** *4 to 5 hours*

1½ **pounds bratwurst links (about 5 or 6)**
1 **can or bottle (12 ounces) beer (not dark)**
1 **medium onion, thinly sliced**
2 **tablespoons packed brown sugar**
2 **tablespoons red wine or cider vinegar**
  Mustard
  Cocktail rye bread

Slow Cooker Directions

1. Combine bratwurst, beer, medium onion, brown sugar and vinegar in slow cooker.

2. Cover; cook on LOW 4 to 5 hours.

3. Remove bratwurst from cooking liquid. Cut into ½-inch-thick slices. For mini open-faced sandwiches, spread mustard on cocktail rye bread. Top with bratwurst slices and onions from slow cooker, if desired. Arrange on platter.

Makes 30 to 36 sandwiches

COOK'S TIP

Choose a light-tasting beer for cooking
brats. Hearty ales might leave the meat
tasting slightly bitter.

Brats in Beer

Mexican-Style Shredded Beef

Prep Time: *12 minutes* / **Cook Time:** *8 to 10½ hours*

    1 tablespoon ground cumin
    1 tablespoon ground coriander
    1 tablespoon chili powder
    1 teaspoon salt
    ½ teaspoon ground red pepper
    1 boneless beef chuck shoulder roast (about 3 pounds), cut in half
    1 cup salsa or picante sauce
    2 tablespoons water
    1 tablespoon cornstarch

Slow Cooker Directions

1. Combine cumin, coriander, chili powder, salt and red pepper in small bowl. Rub over beef. Place ¼ cup of salsa in slow cooker; top with one piece beef. Layer ¼ cup salsa, remaining beef and ½ cup salsa in slow cooker. Cover; cook on LOW 8 to 10 hours or until meat is tender.

2. Remove beef from cooking liquid; cool slightly. Trim and discard excess fat from beef. Using two forks, shred meat.

3. Let cooking liquid stand 5 minutes to allow fat to rise. Skim off fat. To thicken liquid, blend water and cornstarch. Whisk into liquid. Cook, uncovered, on HIGH until thickened. Return beef to slow cooker. Cook 15 to 30 minutes or until hot. Adjust seasonings, if desired. Serve as meat filling for tacos, fajitas or burritos. Leftover mixture may be refrigerated up to 3 days or frozen up to 3 months. *Makes 5 cups filling*

Mexican-Style Shredded Beef

Spicy Asian Pork Filling

Prep Time: *15 to 20 minutes* / **Cook Time:** *8 to 10½ hours*

1 boneless pork sirloin roast (about 3 pounds), cut into 2- to 3-inch
    chunks
½ cup tamari or soy sauce
1 tablespoon chili garlic sauce or chili paste
2 teaspoons minced fresh ginger
2 tablespoons water
1 tablespoon cornstarch
2 teaspoons dark sesame oil

Slow Cooker Directions

1. Combine pork, tamari sauce, chili garlic sauce and ginger in slow cooker;
mix well. Cover; cook on LOW 8 to 10 hours or on HIGH 4 to 5 hours or until
pork is fork tender.

2. Remove roast from cooking liquid; cool slightly. Trim and discard excess
fat. Shred pork using 2 forks. Let liquid stand 5 minutes to allow fat to rise.
Skim off fat.

3. Blend water, cornstarch and sesame oil; whisk into liquid. Cook,
uncovered, on HIGH until thickened. Add shredded meat to slow cooker; mix
well. Cook 15 to 30 minutes or until hot.   *Makes 5½ cups filling*

Spicy Asian Pork Bundles: Place ¼ cup pork filling into large lettuce leaves.
Wrap to enclose. Makes about 20 bundles.

Moo Shu Pork: Lightly spread plum sauce over warm small flour tortillas.
Spoon ¼ cup pork filling and ¼ cup stir-fried vegetables into flour tortillas.
Wrap to enclose. Serve immediately. Makes about 20 tortillas.

Spicy Asian Pork Filling

Chicken Enchilada Roll-Ups

Prep Time: *20 minutes* / **Cook Time:** *7 to 8 hours*

1½ **pounds boneless skinless chicken breasts, each cut lengthwise into 2 or 3 strips**

½ **cup plus 2 tablespoons all-purpose flour, divided**

½ **teaspoon salt**

2 **tablespoons butter**

1 **cup chicken broth**

1 **small onion, diced**

¼ **to** ½ **cup canned jalapeño peppers,* sliced**

½ **teaspoon dried oregano leaves**

2 **tablespoons heavy cream or milk**

6 **flour tortillas (7 to 8 inches)**

6 **thin slices American cheese or American cheese with jalapeño peppers**

*Jalapeño peppers can sting and irritate the skin; wear rubber gloves when handling peppers and do not touch eyes. Wash hands after handling.

Slow Cooker Directions

1. Combine ½ cup flour and salt in resealable plastic food storage bag. Add chicken strips and shake to coat with flour mixture. Melt butter in large skillet over medium heat. Brown chicken strips in batches 2 to 3 minutes per side. Place chicken into slow cooker.

2. Add broth to skillet and scrape up any browned bits. Pour broth mixture into slow cooker. Add onion, jalapeño peppers and oregano. Cover; cook on LOW 7 to 8 hours or on HIGH 3 to 4 hours.

3. Combine remaining 2 tablespoons flour and cream in small bowl; stir to form paste. Stir into chicken mixture; cook on HIGH until thickened. Spoon chicken mixture onto center of flour tortillas. Top with 1 cheese slice. Fold up tortillas and serve.   *Makes 6 servings*

Chicken Enchilada Roll-Up

Barbecued Pulled Pork

1 boneless pork shoulder or butt roast (3 to 4 pounds), trimmed of
    excess fat

1 teaspoon salt

1 teaspoon ground cumin

1 teaspoon paprika

1 teaspoon black pepper

½ teaspoon ground red pepper

1 medium onion, thinly sliced

1 medium green bell pepper, cut into strips

1 bottle (18 ounces) barbecue sauce

½ cup packed light brown sugar

   Sandwich rolls

Slow Cooker Directions

1. Combine salt, cumin, paprika, black pepper and red pepper in small bowl;
rub over roast.

2. Place onion and bell pepper in slow cooker; add pork. Combine barbecue
sauce and brown sugar in medium bowl; pour over meat. Cover; cook on
LOW 8 to 10 hours.

3. Transfer roast to cutting board. Trim and discard fat from roast. Using
2 forks, pull pork into coarse shreds. Serve pork with sauce on sandwich rolls.

Makes 4 to 6 servings

Barbecued Pulled Pork

Slow-Cooked Kielbasa in a Bun

Prep Time: *10 minutes* / **Cook Time:** *7 to 8 hours*

1 pound kielbasa, cut into 4 (4- to 5-inch) pieces
1 large onion, thinly sliced
1 large green bell pepper, cut into strips
¼ teaspoon salt
¼ teaspoon dried thyme leaves
¼ teaspoon black pepper
½ cup chicken broth
4 hoagie rolls, split

Slow Cooker Directions

1. Brown kielbasa in nonstick skillet over medium-high heat 3 to 4 minutes. Place kielbasa in slow cooker. Add onion, bell pepper, salt, thyme and black pepper. Stir in broth.

2. Cover; cook on LOW 7 to 8 hours.

3. Place kielbasa into rolls. Serve with favorite condiments.

Makes 4 servings

COOK'S TIP

For zesty flavor, top sandwiches with pickled
peppers and a dollop of mustard.

METRIC CONVERSION CHART

VOLUME MEASUREMENTS (dry)

1/8 teaspoon = 0.5 mL
1/4 teaspoon = 1 mL
1/2 teaspoon = 2 mL
3/4 teaspoon = 4 mL
1 teaspoon = 5 mL
1 tablespoon = 15 mL
2 tablespoons = 30 mL
1/4 cup = 60 mL
1/3 cup = 75 mL
1/2 cup = 125 mL
2/3 cup = 150 mL
3/4 cup = 175 mL
1 cup = 250 mL
2 cups = 1 pint = 500 mL
3 cups = 750 mL
4 cups = 1 quart = 1 L

VOLUME MEASUREMENTS (fluid)

1 fluid ounce (2 tablespoons) = 30 mL
4 fluid ounces (1/2 cup) = 125 mL
8 fluid ounces (1 cup) = 250 mL
12 fluid ounces (1 1/2 cups) = 375 mL
16 fluid ounces (2 cups) = 500 mL

WEIGHTS (mass)

1/2 ounce = 15 g
1 ounce = 30 g
3 ounces = 90 g
4 ounces = 120 g
8 ounces = 225 g
10 ounces = 285 g
12 ounces = 360 g
16 ounces = 1 pound = 450 g

DIMENSIONS

1/16 inch = 2 mm
1/8 inch = 3 mm
1/4 inch = 6 mm
1/2 inch = 1.5 cm
3/4 inch = 2 cm
1 inch = 2.5 cm

OVEN TEMPERATURES

250°F = 120°C
275°F = 140°C
300°F = 150°C
325°F = 160°C
350°F = 180°C
375°F = 190°C
400°F = 200°C
425°F = 220°C
450°F = 230°C

BAKING PAN SIZES

Utensil	Size in Inches/Quarts	Metric Volume	Size in Centimeters
Baking or Cake Pan (square or rectangular)	8×8×2	2 L	20×20×5
	9×9×2	2.5 L	23×23×5
	12×8×2	3 L	30×20×5
	13×9×2	3.5 L	33×23×5
Loaf Pan	8×4×3	1.5 L	20×10×7
	9×5×3	2 L	23×13×7
Round Layer Cake Pan	8×1½	1.2 L	20×4
	9×1½	1.5 L	23×4
Pie Plate	8×1¼	750 mL	20×3
	9×1¼	1 L	23×3
Baking Dish or Casserole	1 quart	1 L	—
	1½ quart	1.5 L	—
	2 quart	2 L	—